SUPER MARIO™ Series
for Guitar

Alfred

Produced by
Alfred Music Publishing Co., Inc.
P.O. Box 10003
Van Nuys, CA 91410-0003
alfred.com

Printed in USA.

ISBN-10: 0-7390-8280-9
ISBN-13: 978-0-7390-8280-5

Guitar arrangements by Satoshi Aikawa, under supervision by Nintendo.

SUPER MARIO Series ™ for Guitar

CONTENTS

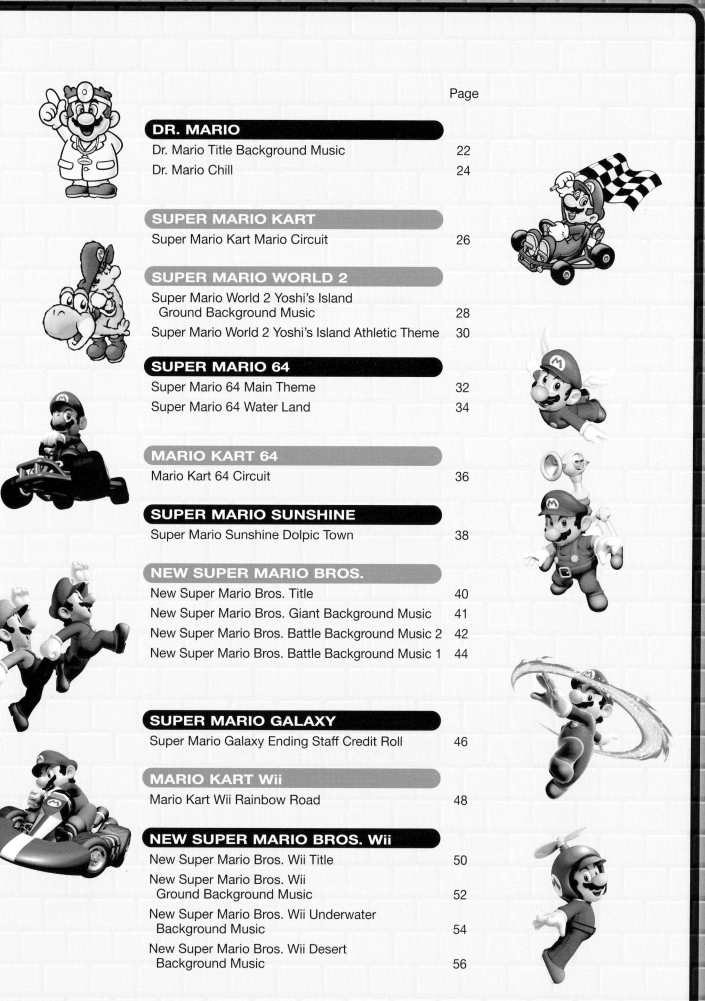

Page

SUPER MARIO BROS.
GROUND BACKGROUND MUSIC

Composed by KOJI KONDO

SUPER MARIO BROS.
UNDERGROUND BACKGROUND MUSIC

Composed by KOJI KONDO

Original Key = C

♩ = 190

N.C.

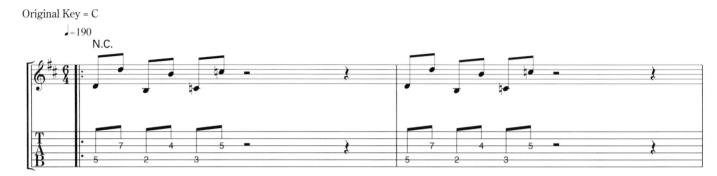

N.C.

N.C.

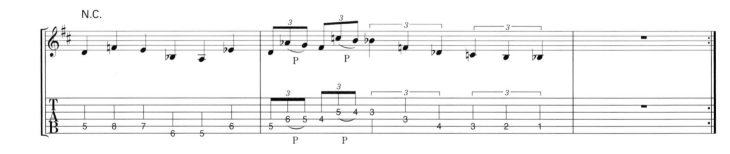

SUPER MARIO BROS.
INVINCIBLE BACKGROUND MUSIC

Composed by KOJI KONDO

Original Key = C

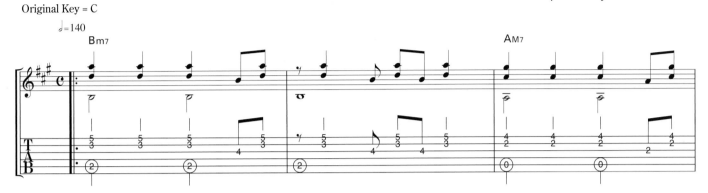

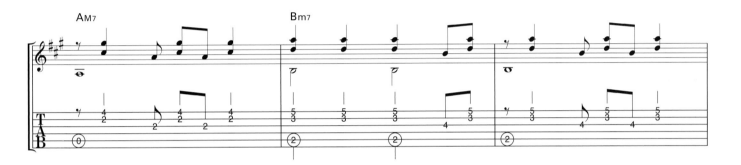

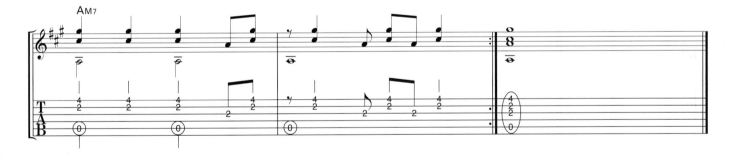

SUPER MARIO BROS.
UNDERWATER BACKGROUND MUSIC

Composed by KOJI KONDO

10

SUPER MARIO BROS.
POWER DOWN, GAME OVER

Composed by KOJI KONDO

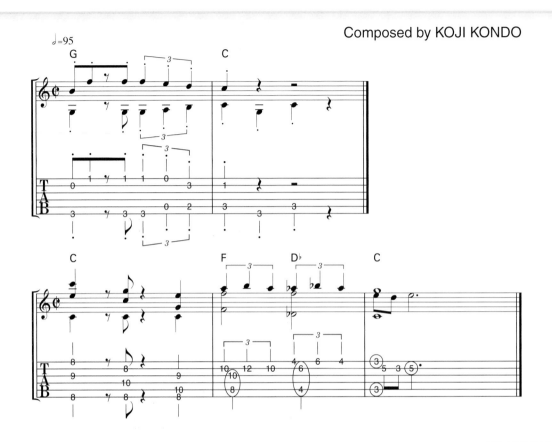

SUPER MARIO BROS.
TIME UP WARNING FANFARE

Composed by KOJI KONDO

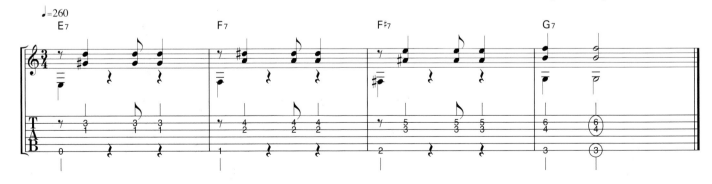

SUPER MARIO BROS.
COURSE CLEAR FANFARE

Composed by KOJI KONDO

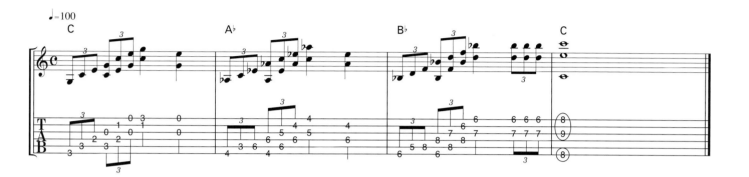

SUPER MARIO BROS.
WORLD CLEAR FANFARE

Original Key = C

Composed by KOJI KONDO

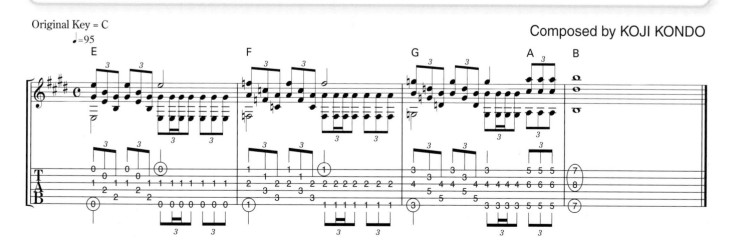

SUPER MARIO BROS. The Lost Levels
THE LOST LEVELS ENDING

Composed by KOJI KONDO

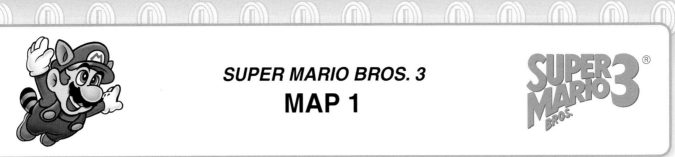

SUPER MARIO BROS. 3
MAP 1

Composed by KOJI KONDO

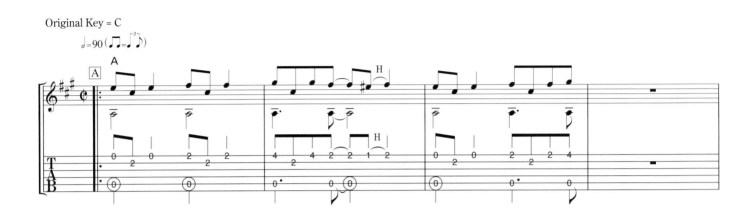

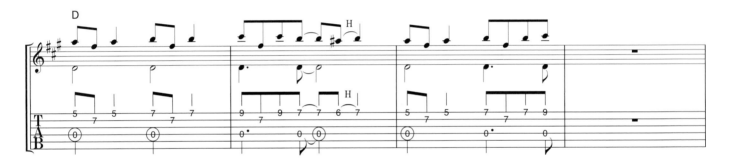

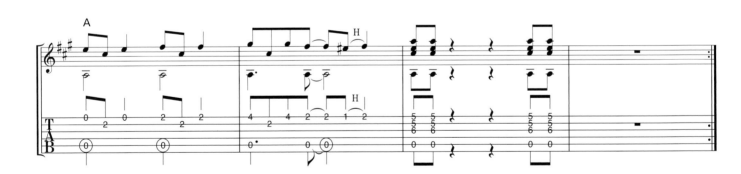

SUPER MARIO BROS. 3
GROUND BACKGROUND MUSIC

Composed by KOJI KONDO

Original Key = C

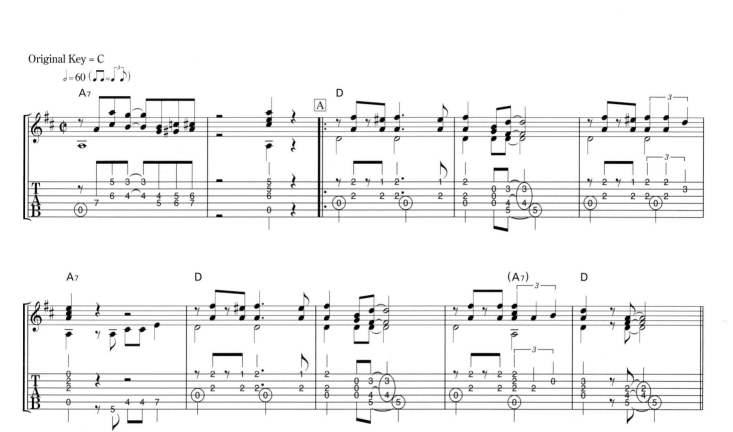

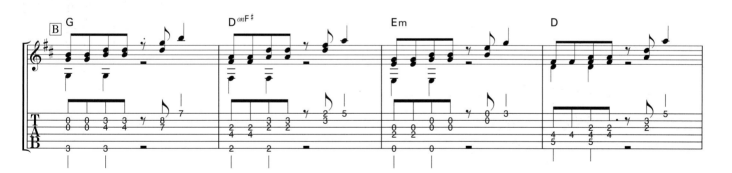

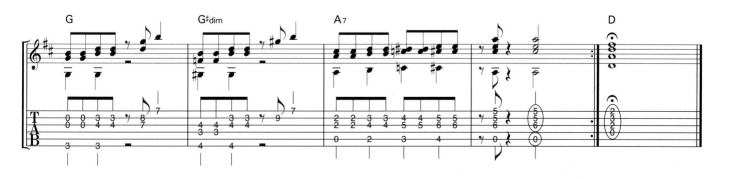

SUPER MARIO BROS. 3
BOSS OF THE FORTRESS

Composed by KOJI KONDO

Original Key = Cm

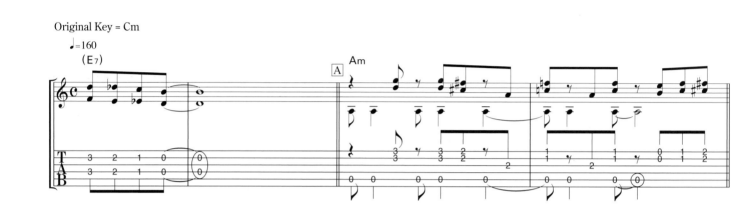

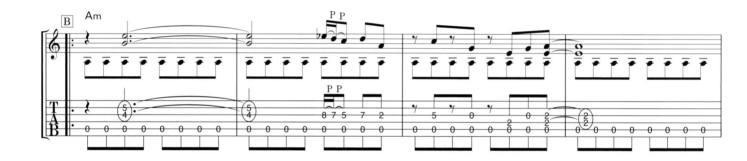

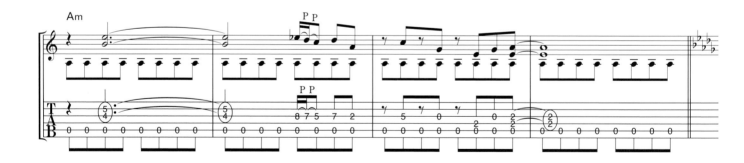

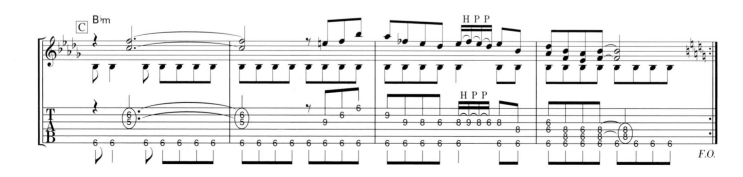

F.O.

SUPER MARIO BROS. 3
SKYSHIP BACKGROUND MUSIC

Composed by KOJI KONDO

Original Key = Bm

$\quad$ = 105

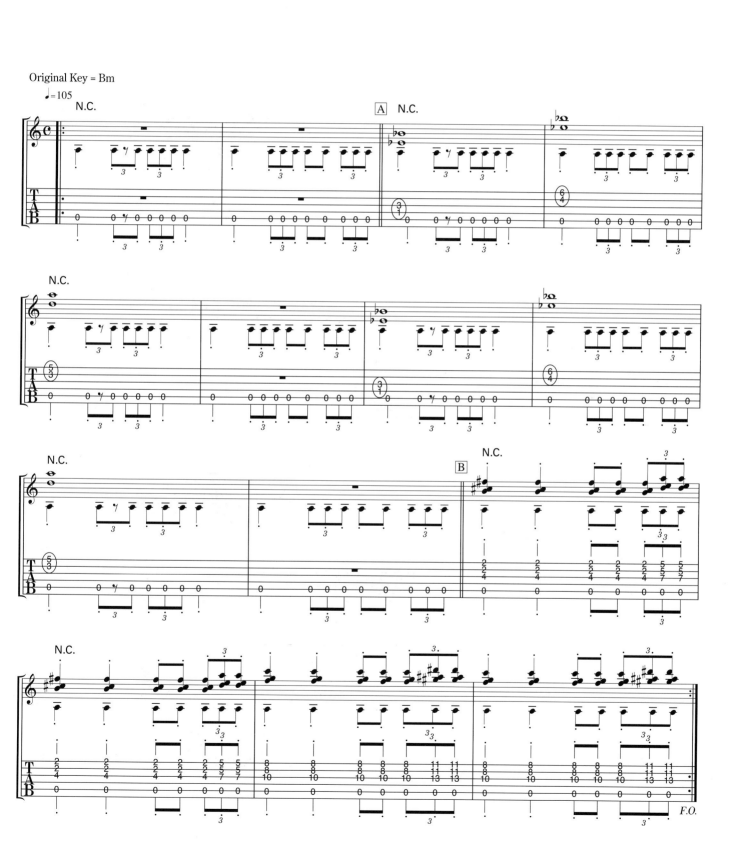

SUPER MARIO WORLD
TITLE

Composed by KOJI KONDO

SUPER MARIO WORLD
CASTLE BACKGROUND MUSIC

Composed by KOJI KONDO

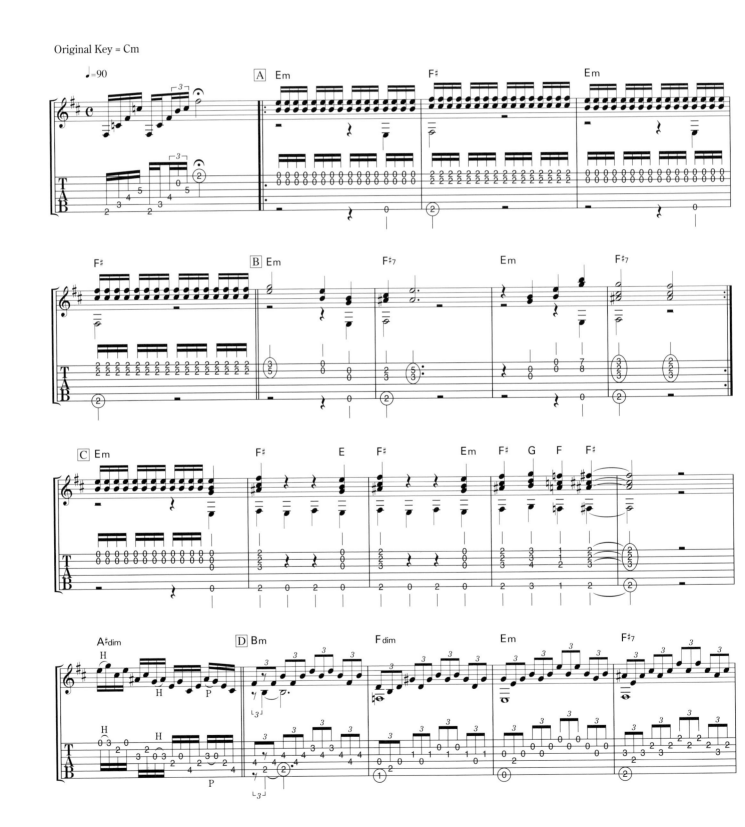

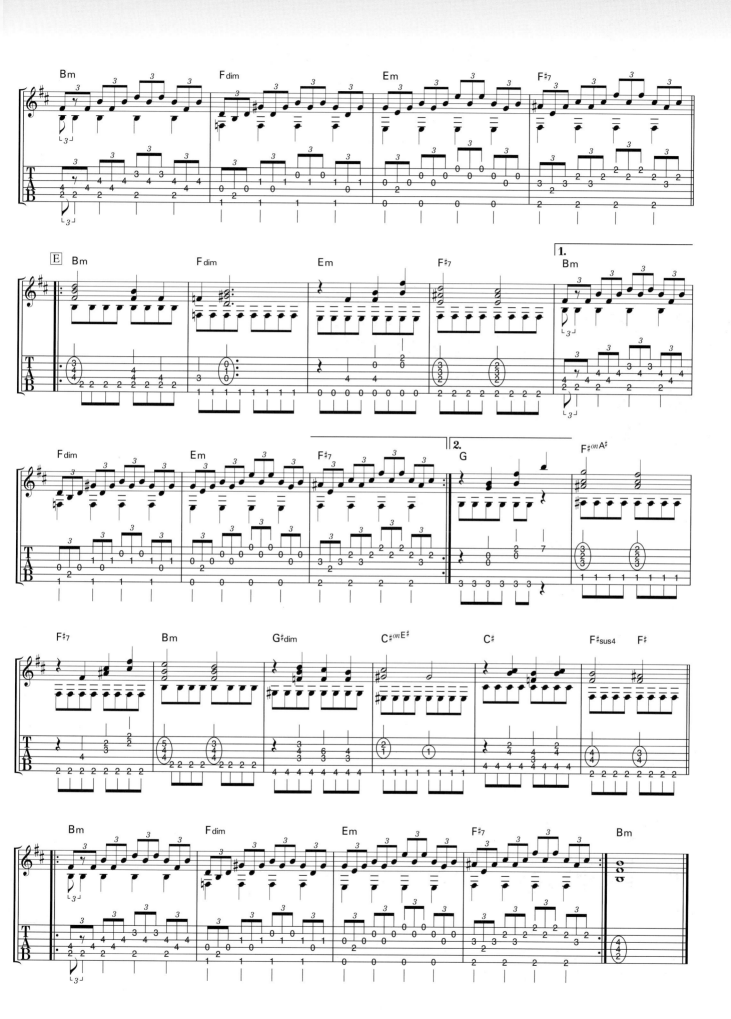

DR. MARIO
TITLE BACKGROUND MUSIC

Composed by HIROKAZU TANAKA

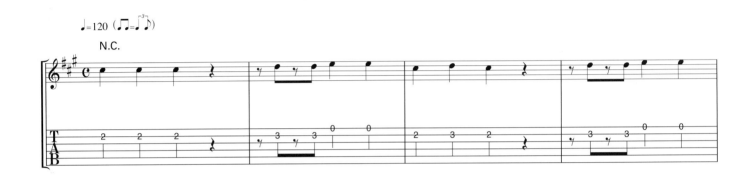

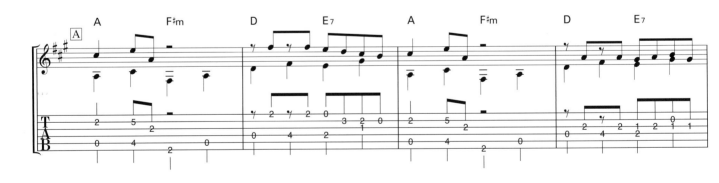

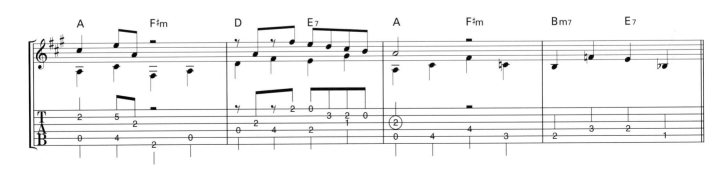

DR. MARIO
CHILL

Composed by HIROKAZU TANAKA

SUPER MARIO KART
MARIO KART CIRCUIT

Composed by SOYO OKA

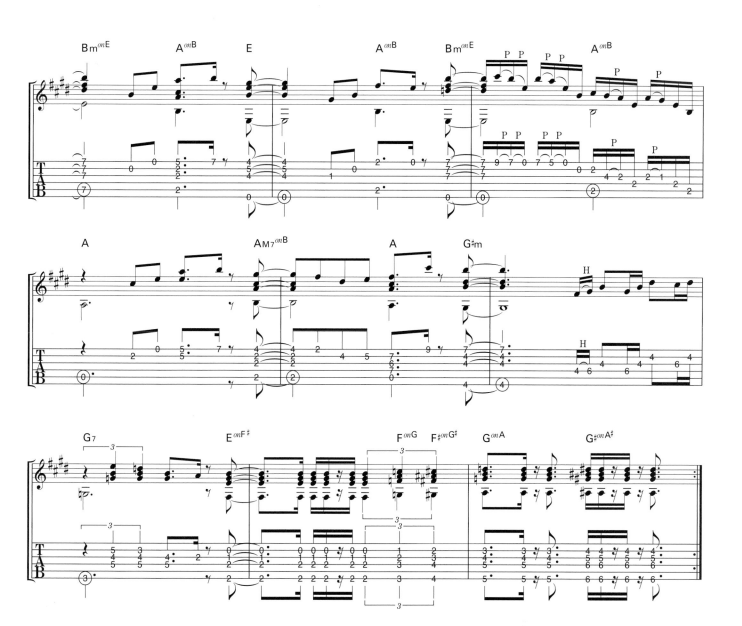

SUPER MARIO WORLD 2
YOSHI'S ISLAND GROUND
BACKGROUND MUSIC

Composed by KOJI KONDO

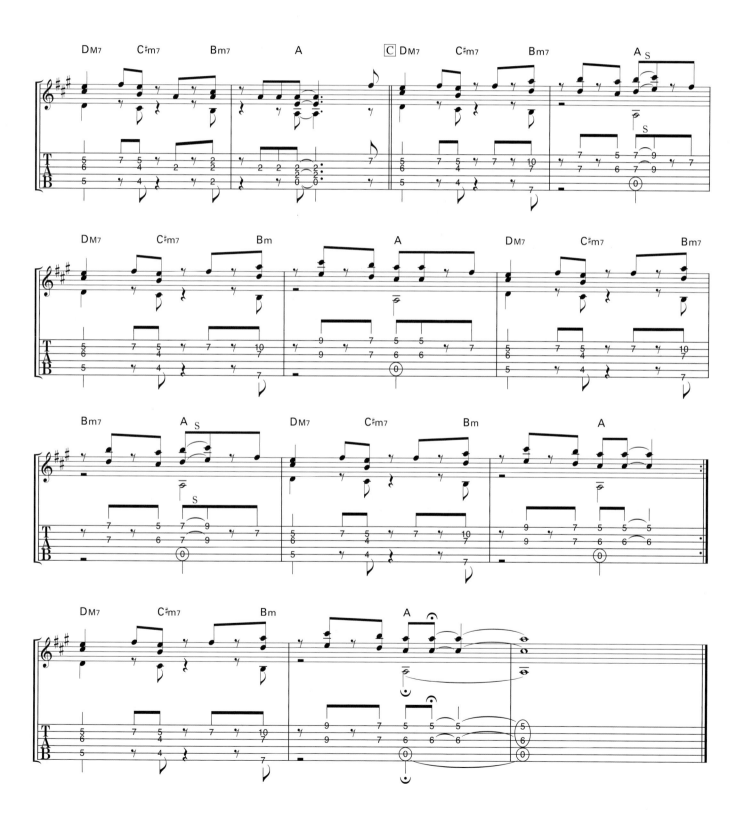

SUPER MARIO WORLD 2
YOSHI'S ISLAND
ATHLETIC THEME

Composed by KOJI KONDO

Original Key = F

SUPER MARIO 64
MAIN THEME

Composed by KOJI KONDO

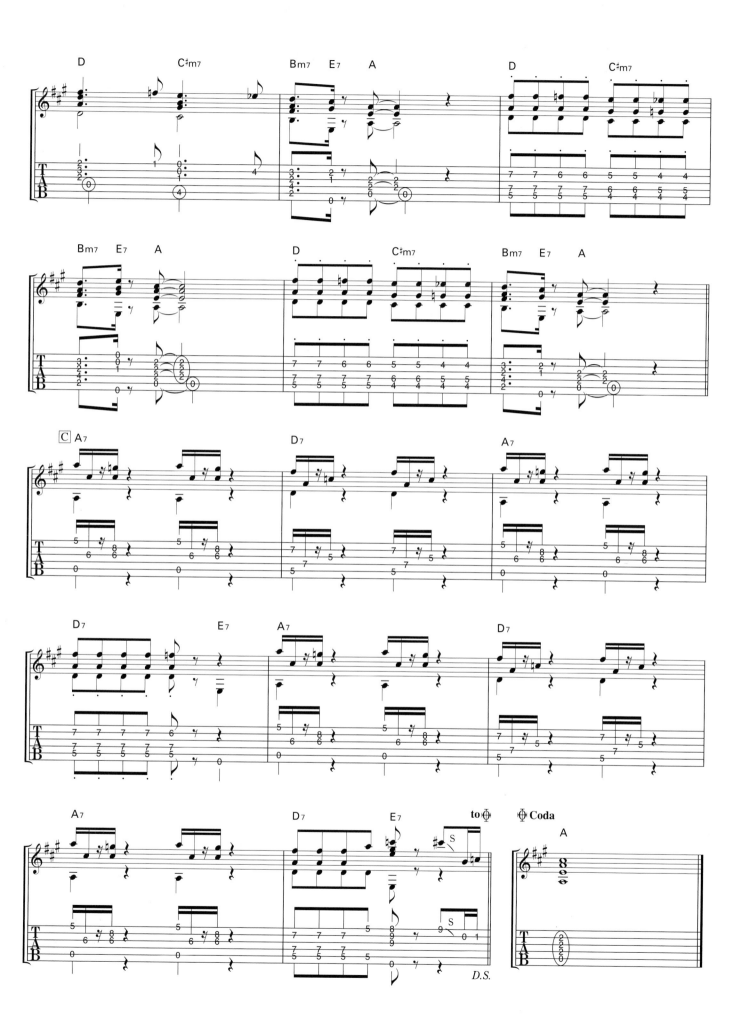

SUPER MARIO 64
WATER LAND

Composed by KOJI KONDO

Original Key = G

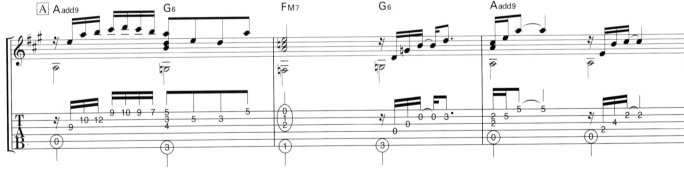

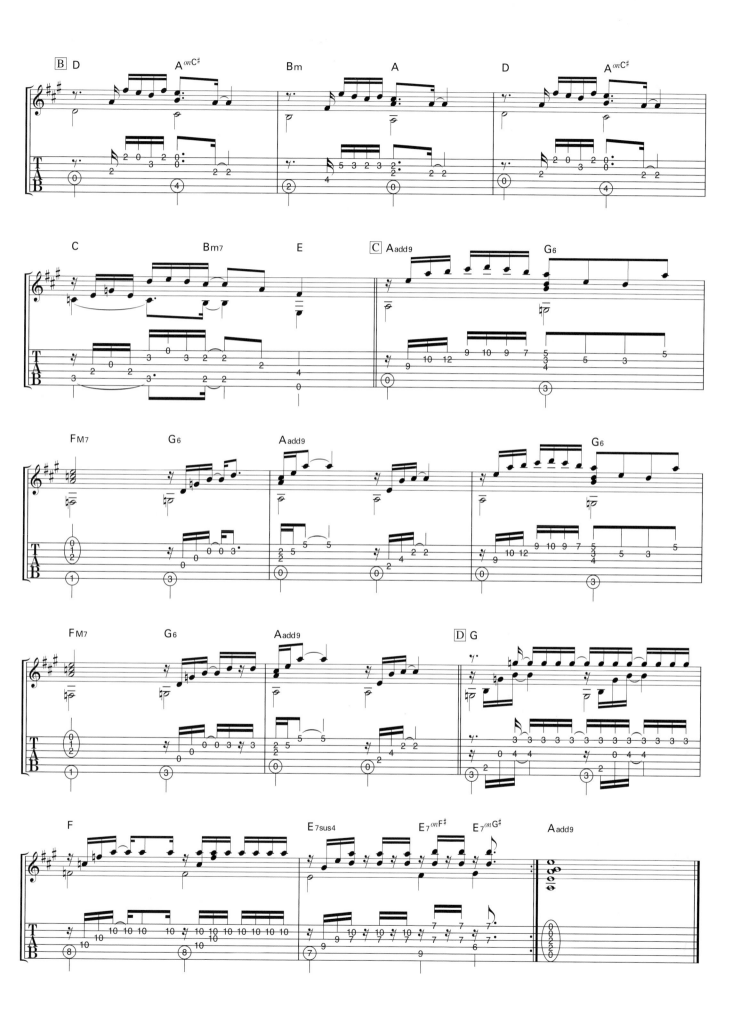

MARIO KART 64
CIRCUIT

Composed by KENTA NAGATA

Original Key = C

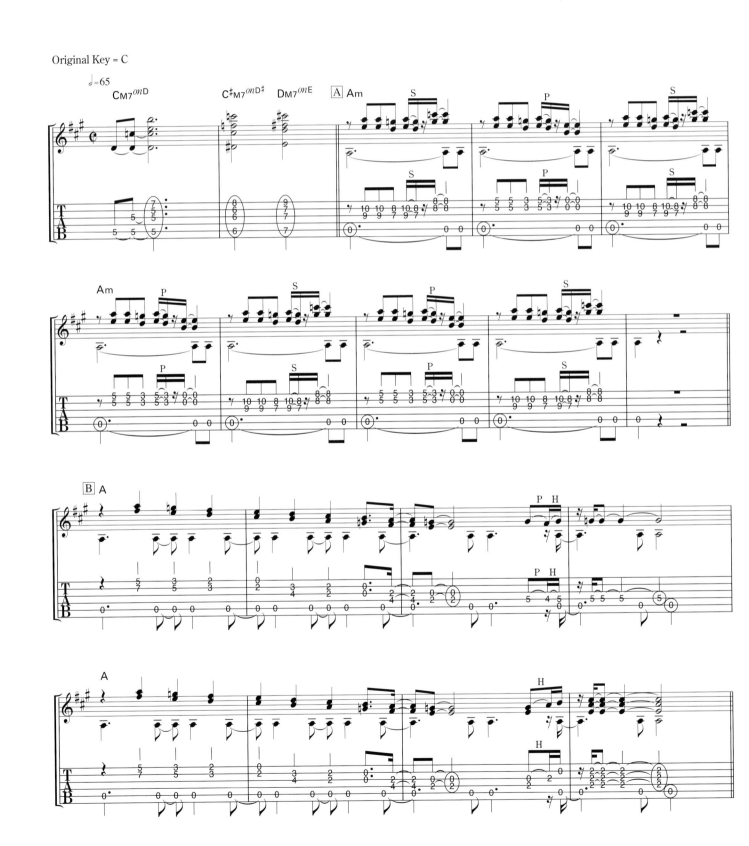

SUPER MARIO SUNSHINE
DOLPIC TOWN

Composed by KOJI KONDO

NEW SUPER MARIO BROS.
TITLE

Composed by ASUKA OHTA

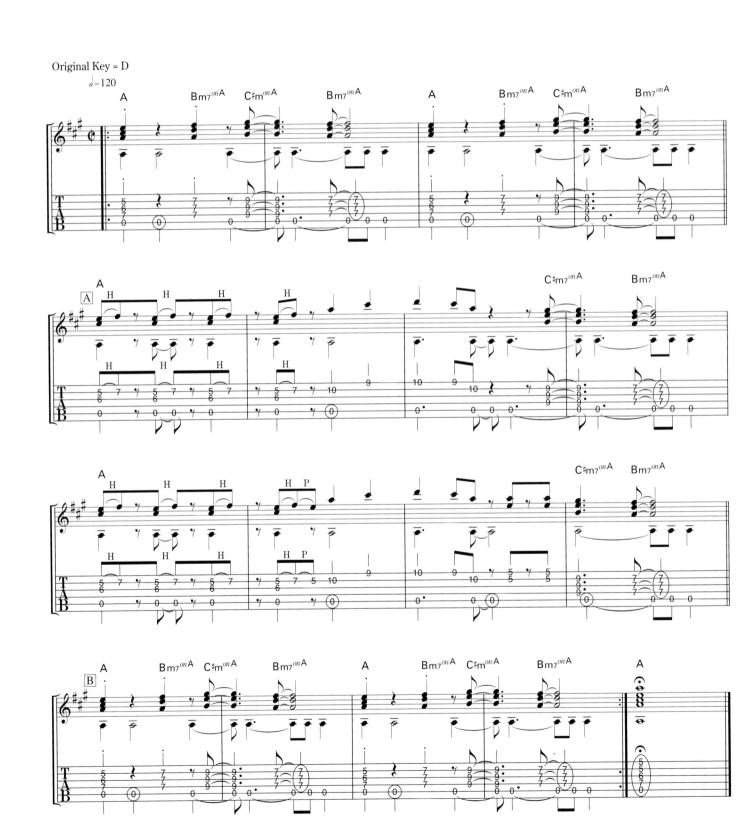

NEW SUPER MARIO BROS.
GIANT BACKGROUND MUSIC

Composed by ASUKA OHTA

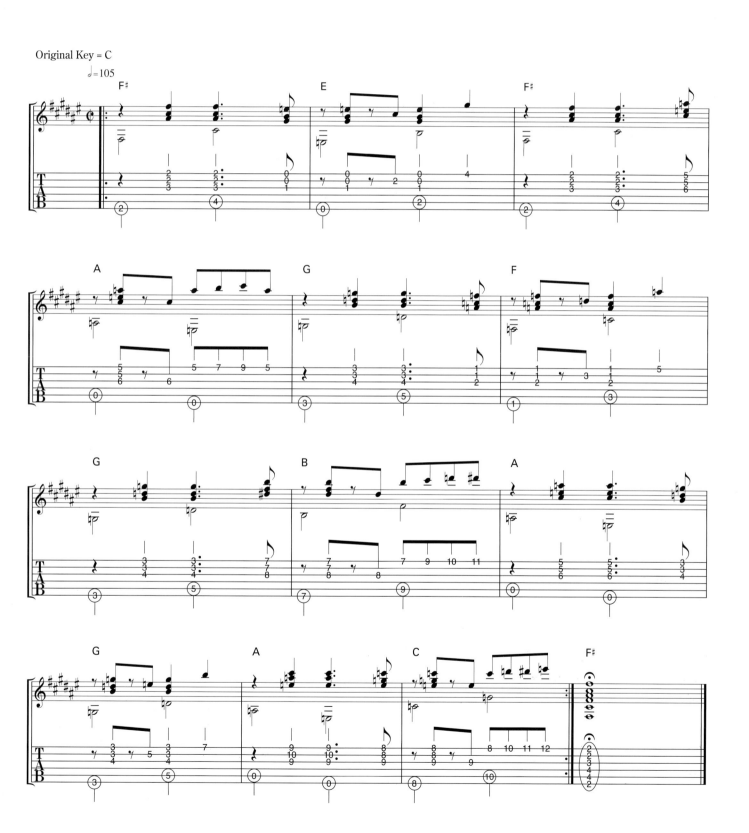

NEW SUPER MARIO BROS.
BATTLE BACKGROUND
MUSIC 2

Composed by KOJI KONDO

NEW SUPER MARIO BROS.
BATTLE BACKGROUND
MUSIC 1

Composed by ASUKA OHTA

SUPER MARIO GALAXY
ENDING STAFF
CREDIT ROLL

Composed by MAHITO YOKOTA

MARIO KART Wii
RAINBOW ROAD

Composed by ASUKA OHTA

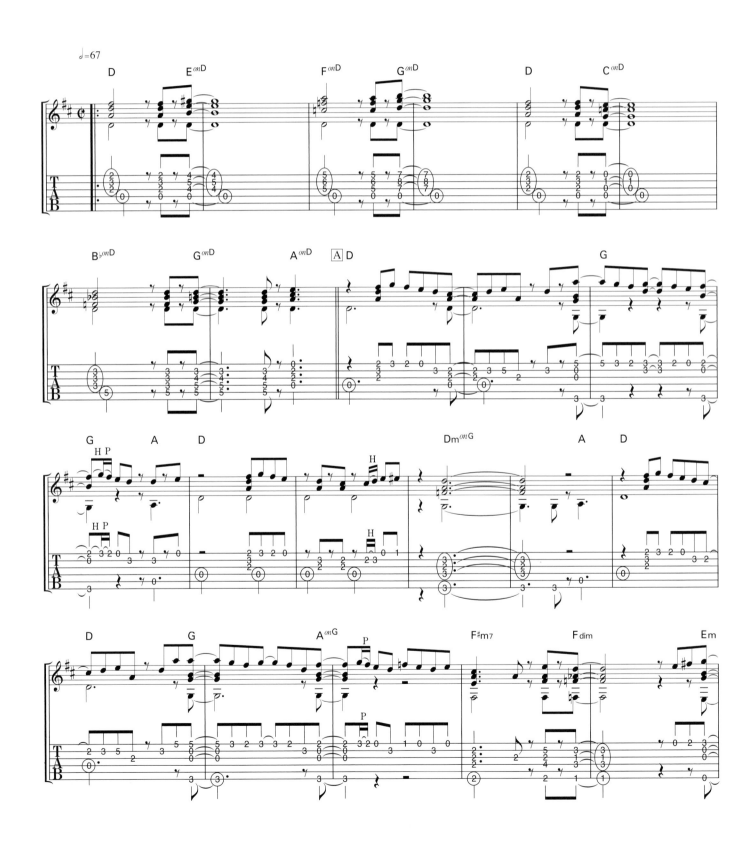

NEW SUPER MARIO BROS. Wii
TITLE

Composed by RYO NAGAMATSU

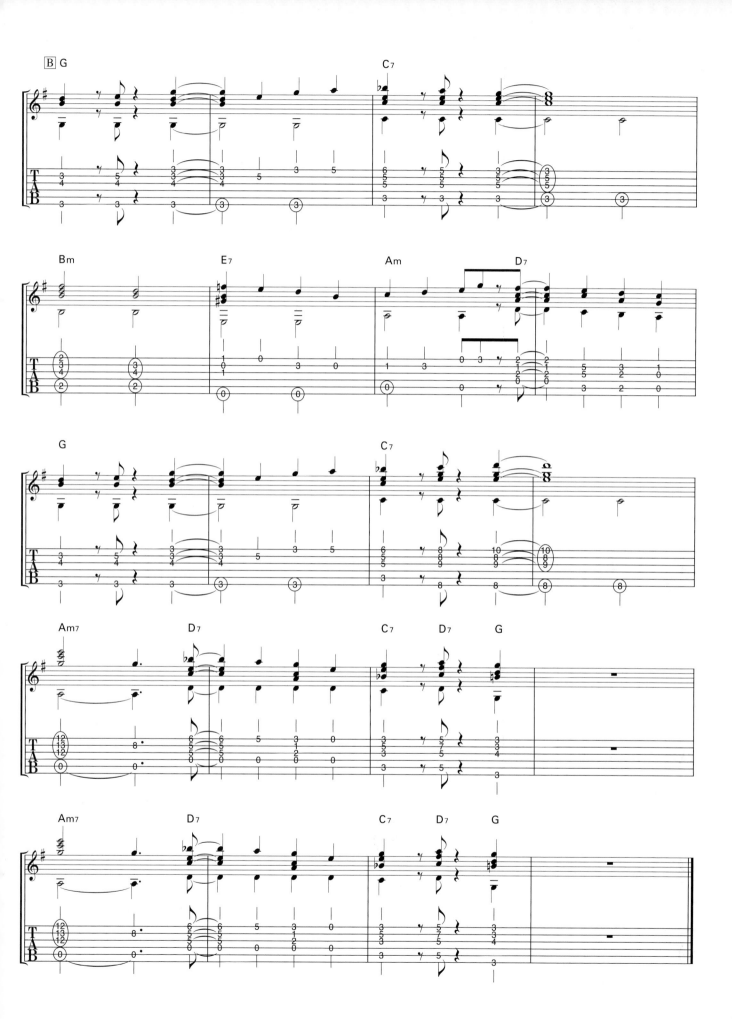

NEW SUPER MARIO BROS. Wii
GROUND
BACKGROUND MUSIC

Composed by KOJI KONDO and KENTA NAGATA

NEW SUPER MARIO BROS. Wii
UNDERWATER BACKGROUND MUSIC

Composed by SHIHO FUJII

NEW SUPER MARIO BROS. Wii
DESERT BACKGROUND MUSIC

Composed by SHIHO FUJII

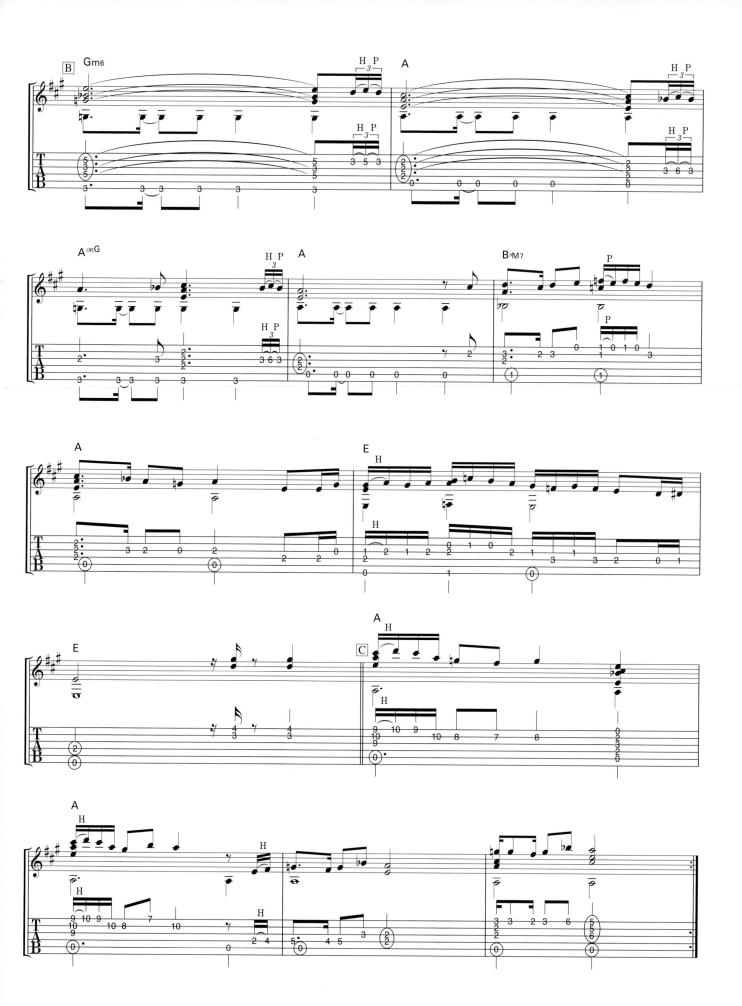

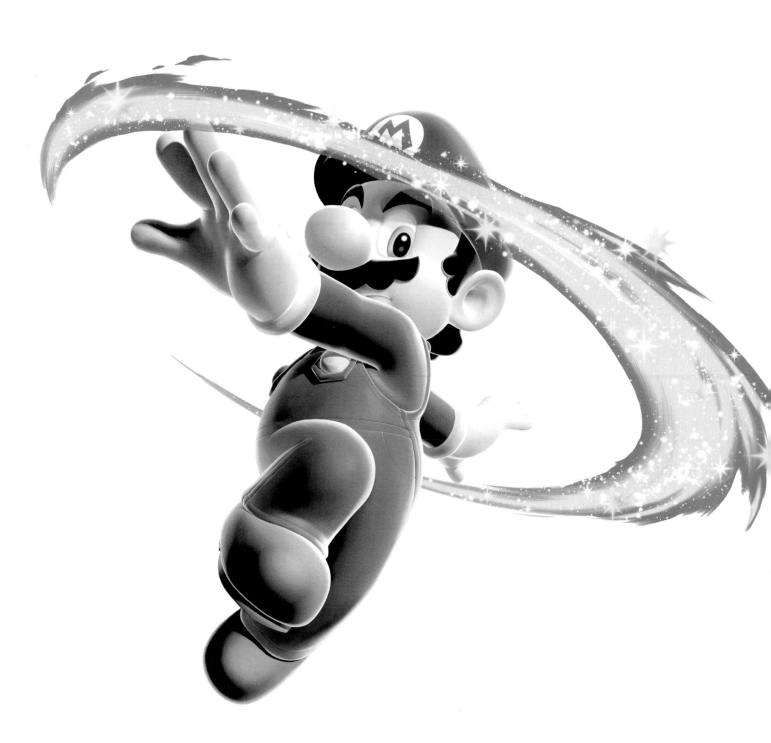